Black Hopelessness

Pastor
Kelly Austin

To order additional copies of this book, contact:
Xlibris
844-714-8691
www.Xlibris.com
Orders@Xlibris.com

ISBN:	Softcover	978-1-6698-4930-8
	EBook	978-1-6698-4929-2

Print information available on the last page

Rev. date: 11/22/2022

Black Hopelessness

Pastor
Kelly Austin

BLACK HOPELESSNESS

Behind the curls, the clothes, the cars, and the music for many black people lies the feeling of hopelessness. They have found the American dream only to be a figurative of the imagination. It appears that things are not getting better but are getting worse. But, before we give up or give in to the feelings of hopelessness, let us pause for a moment and realize that we are a people who have not made it this far by tangible means alone. It hasn't been our money, nor our jobs or our status in the community that has brought us this far, but it's been the hand of God.

THE POLITICAL ARENA

Many young blacks feel the answer to their feelings of hopelessness and helplessness lies in the political arena. They feel if certain candidates are elected this will ensure prosperity, peace, jobs, justice, and hope. As citizens we all should exercise our right to vote and express our political opinions. The old cliché still remains true, "A voteless people is a hopeless people." Many times we see positive results when the right people are elected. Hover, we should not place our entire trust and hope in politics or politicians. We should not fail to realize that the help we can always depend on comes from God. David said in Psalms 146:5-8 "Happy is he that hath the God of Jacob for his help, whose hope is in the Lord his God: which made heaven and earth, the sea, and all that therein is; which executeth judgement for the oppressed; which giveth food to the hungry; the Lord looseth the prisoners; the Lord openth the eyes of the blind; the Lord raiseth them that are bowed down." David assures us that if we place our trust in God that he will provide for us. He also lets us know that God is the answer to what appears to be hopeless.

THE ILLUSIONS

Don't be fooled, the feeling of hopelessness will not just fade away. It did not just magically appear, neither will it magically disappear. Many of our young people have the illusion that success and prosperity will come overnight. Many young black men and women think they will become superstars. They base their hopes on the belief that they will excel in sports and the arts. They identify with people who appear to be successful in these areas. They put themselves in another's place. They fantasize and daydream of fame and fortune. However, the fact is only a very small percentage of athletes and entertainers ever achieve quote success. Most never reach fame and fortune. Even those who have worldly fame and fortune lives often end up a disaster especially when they become wrapped up in materials goods and worldly pleasures. The Bible teaches us in Colossians 3:2 that we are not to set our affections on things on the earth, but we are to set our affection on things above. In other words, on spiritual things such as love, kindness, and peace. The Bible also teaches us in Matthew 6:33 to seek ye first the Kingdom of God and his righteousness, and all these things shall be added unto you. In other words, build hope on nothing less than Jesus Christ and his righteousness, upon that solid rock I'll stand for all other ground in sinking sand.

THE DISGUISE

Many young blacks try to hide their feelings of hopelessness and helplessness behind some type of disguise. Some use dark glasses, gold chains, dark lights, and many of the beauty products designed to improve looks. In other words, oftentimes an attempt s made to cover up the feeling of hopelessness by using products that will make us appear different than what we actually feel. Millions of dollars are spend on products in an attempt to put on an outer cover on what inwardly hurts. Millions of needed dollars are being spent to try and change the outer appearance while the inner man continues to suffer.

Dollars which could be used for food, medicine, and home improvements. Yet This is more easily said than done. Oftentimes reality is most difficult to face and trying to successfully face it without Christ is utterly impossible. For without Christ we can do nothing (John 15:5). But we can do all things through Christ which strengthens us (Phillipians 4:7). That even includes facing reality without makeups or cover-ups which are designed to hide the feeling of hopelessness.

THE ILLEGAL AND THE IMMORAL

We are currently seeing an upward trend of more blacks dealing with their feelings of hopelessness by illegal methods. Methods such as the usage of drugs and the committing of crimes. Although drugs popular and there seems to be an increase usage by all races and cultures, they are not the solution for the feelings of hopelessness. They only provide temporary relief and the pain always returns. God gives complete relief and, for those who trust him, a promise of a better tomorrow. If hopelessness has led you to helplessness and a dependence on drugs, remember Christ's invitation in Matthew 11:28-30 which says, "Come unto me, all ye that labor and are heavy laden, and I will give you rest. Take my yoke upon you and learn of me, for I am meek and lowly in heart; and ye shall find rest unto your souls. For my yoke is easy, and my burden is light." God is simply saying, there is no habit that he can't handle. No problem that he can't solve, ask Him for help.

We are also seeing an increasing number of black men and women participating in acts of immorality. This type of behaviour often increases when one falls into the state of hopelessness. Behaviour such as sex before marriage (fornication), sex while married (adultery) and abortions. Not only can these things harm the body, but they can also destroy the soul. 1 Corinthians 3:16 and 17 says, "Know ye not that ye are the temple of God, that the Spirit of God dwelleth in you? If any man defile the temple of God, him shall God destroy; for the temple of God is holy, which temple ye are." God is saying that the answer to the feeling of hopelessness cannot be quenched through the pleasures of immoral deeds. However, continued immorality can lead to physical and spiritual death.

THE MISUNDERSTOOD

For many young blacks, the feelings of hopelessness stems from their being misunderstood. Oftentimes, blacks are seen by society as being shiftless and lazy. Although this writer in no way attempts to justify laziness, for many young blacks and inability to perform a task. In other words, even before many young blacks are turned down because of their inability to perform, they are turned off because of their inability to express themselves, which causes them to fail to impress others. Therefore, many are not given the chance to do those things which they know how to do. They in turn feel no cares or understands their situation which leaves them in the state of hopelessness and helplessness. But I encourage you not to give up when you are misunderstood, but to look up to the one who understands. David said in Psalms 121:1 "I will lift up mine eyes unto the hills from whence cometh my help." He realized, as we should, that his help comes from the Lord. He realized that Jesus cares, that He made us and He knows all about us. Matthew 10:30 lets us know that Jesus even knows the number of hairs on our head. My brothers and sisters, take all your cares to Jesus, you don't have to worry about your vocabulary being up to par, for God even understands your moans. So when you are misunderstood, take it to Jesus for He understands and He cares for you. Now for those who would be lazy. I invite you to read Proverbs 6:6-11 which says look at the ant, consider her ways and be wise. In other words, examine the character of that ant, how it works even without an overseer or supervisor being present. Then in comparison, my brothers and sisters, let's examine our work habits and see if they measure up. If not, let's make the needed changes realizing that we can do all things through Christ which strengthens us.

THE MIRACULOUS EXPECTATION

For many young and older blacks and feeling of hopelessness and helplessness stems from past miraculous expectations that have failed. For instance, there are many individuals who prey upon others misfortunes to advance their own causes or strictly for their own profit. They state they have miraculous cures for poverty, despair and everything else. They claim if you only purchase their prayer cloth, holy water or praying hands, all of your worries will soon be over. Many young blacks fall for this looking for a quick fix for poverty and loneliness. While many older blacks look for quick recoveries from illness, pains and aches also become easy targets for these individuals. And it's when these promises fail to turn into reality that one is left in a state of hopelessness. This is why it's important that we build our hopes on Jesus alone, nobody but Jesus. As in the words of the song, Jesus can help you, Jesus alone.

BELIEVE
in
MIRACLES

THE QUESTION

The question now my brothers and sisters becomes: for my feelings of hopelessness and helplessness, "Can Jesus be enough?" Is He the answer? Well, I ask you to do as Paul instructed the Corinthians to do in 1 Corinthians 11:28 and II Corinthians 13:5. Examine yourselves, think about all the things you have done trying to find satisfaction for those feelings of hopelessness and helplessness. Think of the things you have done in an attempt to find the answer to what's ailing you. Many of you will find, in most cases, after trying all those things the feelings of depression still exist and a continuation of these feelings puts one in the state of hopelessness. You hear people say try Jesus or give your life to Christ or take your burdens to the Lord and you ask yourself the question "Can Jesus be enough?" Well, sometimes we have to glance backward in order to go forward. History will tell us that most of our foreparents were brought to this country as slaves. It will also tell us that after the Emancipation Proclamation that most were still treated unjustly and unfairly. However, through it all, as the song writer says, they learned to trust in Jesus, they learned to trust in God. Even though outwardly they faced oppression, but those who knew Christ inwardly had joy and peace. The inner man, in turn, became stronger than the outer oppressor. They refused to let oppression or anything else leave them in a state of hopelessness. For they had faith in God. They probably depended on passages of scripture such as "Greater is he that is in me than he tha is in the world (1 John 4:4), I can do all things through Christ which strengtheneth me (Philippians 4:13). We are more than conquerors through Him that loved us (Romans 8:3). But the greatest encouragement for our Christian foreparents probably came from the words spoke by Jesus in Matthew 28:20 "...and lo I am with you always eve unto the end of the world." And that's the reason, even through oppression, they could sing song like "I've got Jesus and That's Enough." He was enough to give them the inspiration and the aspiration to continue upward working for a better tomorrow.

THE ANSWER

The answer is yes, Jesus is enough for us today as He was for our foreparents yesterday. Yes, we must put our faith and trust in Him. Yes, He will give us the victory over what appears to be a hopeless situation. The writer wishes to pause at this point to show you how to be saved. Because for some, the Spirit of God may be moving upon their hearts right now to accept Jesus Christ as their personal Saviour. Those of you who have a Bible present, open it up to Romans 3:33 and it will read "For all have sinned and come short of the glory of God." That includes you and I. Now turn to Romans 5:8 which reads "But God commendeth His love toward us, in that, while we were yet sinners, Christ died for us." In other words, God recognized our condition as sinners, yet he had such great love for us that He sent His son, Jesus, to die for us. St. John 3:16 says "For God so loved the world that He gave His only begotten Son, that whosoever believeth in Him should not perish, but have everlasting life." Now turn to Romans 6:23 which reads "For the wages of sin is death but the gift of God is Eternal Life through Jesus Christ." You and I were born in sin and shaped in inequity (wickedness), Psalms 51:5 Now because of man (mankind) being sinful and God being holy, in order for man to reach God, His law required an atonement, in other words, a perfect sacrifice. Since the first man, Adam, had sinned and all others were born in sin, there was none who could be that perfect sacrifice. There was one who could pay the price required because of man's sins. So God sent His only begotten Son, Jesus Christ, a perfect sacrifice (II Corinthians 5:21; I Peter 1:18-19) to be an atonement for our sins in order that we might be saved. For God sent not His son into the world to condemn the world, but that the world through him might be saved (St. John 3:17). So right now, if you want to be saved and the Spirit of God is moving on your heart to try Jesus, don't worry about the proper words to say, just cry out to Jesus and in childlike faith ask Him to come into your life. The Bible says in Romans 10:9 that if thou confess with thy mouth the Lord Jesus and shalt believe in thine heart that God hath raised Him from the dead, thou shalt be saved. Romans 10:13 also says, for whosoever shall call upon the name of the Lord be saved. You can do it right now even in the state of hopelessness.

THE HOPE WORTH SUFFERING FOR

A few days ago i read a Sunday School lesson which was entitled "A Hope Worth Suffering For." We stated earlier in this book that hopelessness would not just disappear, neither will suffering. Even if you accept Christ into your heart and receive Him as our personal Saviour, this does not mean that everything around you will automatically change. However it does mean that you will begin to see things differently. In other words, you will begin to see things as Jesus sees them. Also, you will better understand why there is so much poverty, disease, crime and violence all around us today, why there is still prejudice, injustice and corruption. However, the good part is, the part that you will not be able to logically understand is that through it all, with Christ you can have peace and joy. The Bible says in Phillippians 4:7 "...and the peace of God, which passeth all understanding, shall keep your hearts and minds through Christ Jesus. You will realize that the joy and peace you have the world didn't give to you and the world can't take it away. For Jesus said in St. John 14:27 "Peace I leave with you, my peace I give unto you, not as the world giveth give I unto you. "Romans 14:17 says "For the Kingdom of God is not meat and drink, but righteousness and peace and joy in the Holy Ghost. Before we go any further we do want to re-emphasize that just because you have accepted Christ does not exclude you from suffering. But those who are truly living for Him will see the cause of their suffering changing from negative reasons to positive ones. My brothers and sisters, I want you to know there is a difference between suffering for wrong doing than suffering for doing what's right. The Bible says in 1 Peter 3:14 "If ye suffer for righteousness sake, happy are ye and be not afraid of their terror neither be troubled." In other words, when you suffer "...we shall also reign with Him." And don't be surprised if things around you begin to change. For Jesus said in Matthew 19:26 "...with God all things are possible."

THE FINALITY

And finally the feeling of hopelessness and helplessness is not restricted to blacks alone. Its presence is felt in all races, but the good news is that Jesus loves us all and that through him any man, woman, boy or girl can have the victory over the feeling of hopelessness. For God has no respect of persons. And after accepting Christ as your personal Saviour, pray and ask God to direct you to a Spirit-filled church where you can continue to grow in the knowledge of our Lord and Saviour Jesus Christ.

The End

ROMANS 8:24-28, 35-39

24 For we are saved by hope: but hope that is seen is not hope: for what a man seeth, why doth he yet hope for?

25 But if we hope for that we see not, then do we with patience wait for it.

26 Likewise the Spirit also helpeth our infirmities: for we know not what we should pray for as we ought: but the Spirit itself maketh intercession for us with groanings which cannot be uttered.

27 And he that searcheth the hearts knoweth what is the mind of the Spirit, because he maketh intercession for the saints according to the will of God.

28 And we know that all things work together for good to them that love God, to them who are the called according to his purpose.

35 Who shall separate us from the love of Christ? shall tribulation, or distress, or persecution, or famine, or nakedness, or peril, or sword?

36 As it is written, For thy sake we are killed all the day long; we are accounted as sheep for the slaughter.

37 Nay, in all these things we are more than conquerors through him that loved us.

38 For I am persuaded, that neither death, nor life, nor angels, nor principalities, nor powers, nor things present, nor things to come,

39 Nor height, nor depth, nor any other creature, shall be able to separate us from the love of God, which is in Christ Jesus our Lord.

ROMANS 12:17-21

17 Recompense to no man evil for evil. Provide things honest in the sight of all men.

18 If it be possible, as much as lieth in you, live peaceably with all men.

19 Dearly beloved, avenge not yourselves, but rather give place unto wrath: for it is written, Vengeance is mine; I will repay, saith the Lord.

20 Therefore if thine enemy hunger, feed him; if he thirst, give him drink: for in so doing thou shalt heap coals of fire on his head.

21 Be not overcome of evil, but overcome evil with good.

II CORINTHIANS 4:6-9, 17-18

6 For God, who commanded the light to shine out of darkness, hath shined in our hearts, to give the light of the knowledge of the glory of God in the face of Jesus Christ.

7 But we have this treasure in earthen vessels, that the excellency of the power may be of God, and not of us.

8 We are troubled on every side, yet not distressed; we are perplexed, but not in despair;

9 Persecuted, but not forsaken; cast down, but not destroyed;

17 For our light affliction, which is but for a moment, worketh for us a far more exceeding and eternal weight of glory;

18 While we look not at the things which are seen, but at the things which are not seen: for the things which are seen are temporal; but the things which are not seen are eternal.

TITUS 2:11-15

11 For the grace of God that bringeth salvation hath appeared to all men,

12 Teaching us that, denying ungodliness and worldly lusts, we should live soberly, righteously, and godly, in this present world;

13 Looking for that blessed hope, and the glorious appearing of the great God and our Saviour Jesus Christ;

14 Who gave himself for us, that he might redeem us from all iniquity, and purify unto himself a peculiar people, zealous of good works.

15 These things speak, and exhort, and rebuke with all authority. Let no man despise thee.

ST. JOHN 16:33

33 These things I have spoken unto you, that in me ye might have peace. In the world ye shall have tribulation: but be of good cheer; I have overcome the world.

Printed in the United States
by Baker & Taylor Publisher Services